ICO

The Ultimate Guide to Investing In ICOs

Ikuya Takashima

Copyright © 2018 Ikuya Takashima

All rights reserved.

ISBN:198618210X
ISBN-13:9781986182102

CONTENTS

Introduction i

Chapter one: A Brief Look At Blockchain Technology 1

Chapter Two: Introduction To ICOs 5

Chapter Three: The Advantages And Disadvantages Of Investing In ICOs 15

Chapter Four: What Makes For A Great ICO? 23

Chapter Five:: What Do ICO Scams Look Like? 30

Chapter six: How Do I Know That The White paper Is Any Good? 38

Chapter Seven: It's All About Teamwork 46

Chapter Eight: How To Evaluate The ICO's Market Projections And Competitor Analyses 51

Chapter Nine: Evaluating The Business Model 60

Chapter Ten: Keep A Legal Eye On Things 73

Chapter Eleven: Technical Aspects Of Investing 76

Chapter Twelve: Getting Down To Business 86

Chapter Thirteen: Keeping Yourself Safe From Fraudsters 98

Chapter Fourteen: Your Cheat Sheet Of Sites 103

Final Words 106

Other Ikuya Takashima books available on Amazon .. 108

About The Author 109

Introduction

Congratulations on purchasing this book!

Have you been wondering about the exciting world of cryptocurrency and looking for a way to get a piece of the action? Trading these currencies can be lucrative but keeping up with market fluctuations, transaction costs, and so on can be very difficult.

Which currencies are worth investing in? How do you know? The truth is that trading cryptocurrency is not for the faint of heart and requires a lot of expertise in the area.

It's true that you could stand to gain a lot of money, but you could lose it just as quickly. If only there were a better way of getting in on the ground floor of the crypto market.

There is. Instead of trying to figure out when the best time to buy and sell currency is, you can put your investment to good use, support a project that you believe in, and stand to make a killing as well.

Initial Coin Offerings are an excellent way to dip your toes in the water. Get in as early as possible and, if you have chosen correctly, you will be laughing all the way to the bank in a few months or years when the project is complete.

The key is in choosing the right ICO to invest in and that requires some specialist knowledge. Some projects sound great on paper but are difficult to execute, some ICOs never reach their full potential because they are unable to attract enough investors, and some are out and out scams. Very few ICOs move on to achieve meteoric success.

How do you choose a project with the best chance of success? I am not going to lie to you – there is no two-step formula to see whether the project is a good investment or not. You are going to have to do your research carefully, ahead of time, but the rewards are well worth the effort.

Choose the right ICO, and you could be set up for life. And here's a secret, it's not that hard to choose the right ICO if you are willing to put in the effort upfront.

In this book, I am going to teach you how you can make the right investment decisions. I will show you how to look at the ICO from every angle you can think of – from the team behind it to the potential pitfalls of the investment.

By the time you are finished here, you will know as much, if not more about the ICO than the team itself and will be poised to make the right decision.

In this book, we go through how to find ICOs to invest in, how to vet them properly, how to work out what their potential for growth is and how to know whether they are on the right track, all so that you can make your investments with complete confidence.

There is no such thing as a sure thing in the world of ICOs, but this book will help you find the closest thing possible.

IKUYA TAKASHIMA

Are you ready to make some money?

Chapter one: A Brief Look At Blockchain Technology

In this chapter, you will learn a little about how blockchain technology works. The ICOs that we are talking about in this book are all based on blockchain technology, so we are going to do a quick run-through of what the blockchain is and how it works. If you already know how the blockchain operates, you *can* skip through to Chapter 2, however, it may not be a bad idea to refresh yourself here.

What Is The Blockchain?

Basically, it is a network of computers that all run the software for any particular blockchain. Each computer in the network is known as a node, and each node contains the information related to the system. So, we are essentially talking about a distributed ledger.

The advantage of this is that it is highly secure and that the information contained therein is never controlled by a single entity. The data cannot be lost or destroyed unless every node is also destroyed. This is great for server availability. Even if half the nodes went down at the same time, the system would still continue to operate.

There are other advantages as well. It is one step closer to a supercomputer because it gives users access to the computing power over the whole network. One ICO that did very well was Golem. With Golem, you can rent the computing power of others in the network to supplement your own. They benefit because they are paid, and you benefit because you don't need to upgrade your hardware.

The blockchain is permanent. The data is stored in blocks, with each new block containing information that links it to the previous block. The data is signed and timestamped. To add any transactions, you need to sign them with your private key and then submit them to the network.

The transactions then undergo a verification process by 'miners'. These are people on the network that allow the software to run on their systems and actively allow their computers to solve complex algorithmic equations. These equations are designed to ensure that the transaction is signed correctly.

The miner that comes up with a solution that can be verified first is rewarded for their efforts in cryptocurrency.

It is only once the information is verified that it becomes part of the chain.

The security of the chain lies in the fact that it cannot be changed. In order to alter a particular piece of data in the chain, you would also need to change any blocks that came after it as well. Every change would have to be approved by the nodes, or computers within the network. This would mean a hacker would have to access all the nodes within the network at the same time.

What Is Ethereum?

There are many different applications that run on blockchain technology, like Bitcoin, Ripple, and Ethereum. Blockchain technology is opensource, so many applications have been developed with blockchain at their core.

In this book, we focus on Ethereum because that is where you will find most of the ICOs.

Ethereum goes beyond a simple ledger – it has programming language at its core and so enables users to create dapps and smart contracts.

What Are Dapps?

These are decentralized applications. The advantage of creating them on this platform is that they can be sold directly to the end user. For many ICOs, the project that they are hoping you will invest in is a dapp.

What Is A Smart Contract?

This is a piece of programming that works on a simple 'if this, then that' basis. So, for our purposes it would go something like:

If one Ether is received, then X number of tokens are sent back.

What Is Ether?

Ether acts as both a type of cryptocurrency and a way to pay for services within Ethereum. Every transaction carried out on Ethereum must be paid for in Ether or Gas. The more complex the transaction, the higher the cost will be.

Chapter Summary

There is a lot more that we could talk about when it comes to blockchain technology, but these are the basics that you need for now.

In this chapter you have learned:

Chapter Two: Introduction To ICOs

An Initial Coin Offering or ICO is essentially a way that companies use to raise funds to aid development or to get the project off the ground – they are swapping their cryptocurrency for the whatever cryptocurrency the investor is using. An initial coin offering is run while the project is still in its development stages and so the tokens are not going to be worth much at the time.

The investors are betting that the company will be successful and looking to make a significant return on investment.

The best way to think of this is a crowdfunding exercise rather than an outright sale of stock. You can trade them on a coin exchange like Poloniex if they have been listed, but not all companies give token holders voting rights.

These are classified as high-risk investments because there is usually no working model or assets when you invest. It's a lot like a venture capital investment.

Fun Facts About ICO's

- ICOs have raised more startup capital for companies using blockchain technology than venture capitalists have. At the date of writing this, more than $2 billion has been raised in the manner. Not too shabby for the new kid on the block, is it?
- Ethereum's ICO can be classified as the starting point for ICOs in general. It was the first time that companies had raised money this way and the software developed made it possible for other businesses to do the same. Ethereum was forward-thinking. They gave users more reasons to use the network, aside from just transferring assets or mining for coin.
- Most ICOs are based on tokens issued on the Ethereum blockchain because Ethereum makes it easy to create your own tokens and cryptocurrency. Tokens issued in this way are known as ERC-20.
- Augur, Golem, and Melonport are all examples of ERC-20 tokens.

- The DAO raised over $150 million on Ethereum – still, the record for the most money raised. Unfortunately, it ended up being a failure because this app got hacked due to a security flaw in the smart contract it set up and this allowed some of the money raised to be stolen.
- It was because of this hack that you now have both Ethereum and Ethereum Classic. The majority of users decided to start a new chain that branched off from the original just before the hack occurred so that it was like the funds were never stolen. This branch is still called Ethereum. The few purists on the site felt that they should continue as is, despite the money that was lost and didn't change over to the new branch. This is known as Ethereum Classic. For this book, we are working on Ethereum. When buying Ether, make sure it is for Ethereum and not Ethereum Classic.
- It is not only start-ups that can use this form of funding. The established company, Kik, also entered the arena as a way of raising more working capital.

Two Types Of ICOs

- **Currency ICOs**: This is where a new form of cryptocurrency is developed. The company benefits because they receive funds that they can use during the development stage. The investor benefits because they get in at the ground level. If the project becomes popular, the tokens will increase in value. Bitcoin is an excellent example of this type. When it comes to a token that is solely a cryptocurrency, you need to be careful. For starters, it may be viewed as a security rather than a digital product and so will be prone to stricter regulation. Secondly, it is simple to make a cryptocurrency of your own - Ethereum even provides a template to do so. That means that there are a lot out there that are entirely worthless.

- **Project ICOs**: A project ICO is a token that will allow you to have certain rights within the program. This could be in the form of voting rights, like with Augur, or it could be payment for using the program or features within it. Ether was initially created to pay for using the network but has also evolved into a robust cryptocurrency in its own right.

Dynamic or Static Funding For ICOs

- **Dynamic funding**: In this instance, the tokens are not issued with a predetermined value and so the more that are sold, the higher the price becomes.

- **Static funding**: This is where the developers have a specific funding goal and create tokens that have a value that is predetermined. The value is not going to change while the ICO is running.

It is also possible for companies to create a new token once another has been sold, but they will usually have a predetermined limit for how many times they are able to do this.

Investment Value Of ICOs

There has been a lot of buzz about cryptocurrency investments, and ICO investments as well. One particular market segment that has shown a lot of interest here is the venture capitalist investor.

This type of investing is perfect for them – you get in at the ground level, leave the day to day running of the company and product development to someone else and stand to make a fortune if the company becomes highly successful.

For standard investors, however, it is this "if" that becomes a large part of the problem. The industry is largely unregulated, and this is another thing that can make investors nervous. Also, some investors feel that the ICOs are overvalued and that the bubble is bound to burst.

It can, however, be very lucrative – who here wishes that they had gotten in on the ICO of Ethereum where you could pick up Ether for a few cents? Ethereum raised more than $80 million during the ICO phase, and so was a perfect example of how popular this kind of investment is. Considering that they are now trading at between $750 and $1100 per token, you have some idea of how good the investment return could be.

Now, before you rush off and buy any ICO you can find, I need to warn you – this is still a high-risk investment. If you rush into it blind and let yourself be blown away by great advertising or a flashy website, without checking into it any further, you could lose everything.

It is not all doom and gloom, though, if you do your due diligence on the ICO before investing, you could stand to make a tidy sum of money.

What To Look For Before Investing

We are going to go through this in more detail at a later stage but, for now, here are some basics to consider:

- Ignore the flashy website and claims about being the best thing to ever hit the blockchain market. Every company will make claims like this, it might be true, but it also might be a marketing ploy. Also, even if the idea is fantastic, there is no guarantee that they are going to get it right. A popular story that can be applied here is that of Thomas Edison and the light bulb. It was a brilliant idea, but it took hundreds of tries before he actually got it right. Is the company you are looking into going to be as persistent?

- Look at the team itself – what history do they have, what experience do they have? Does it make sense for this group of people to be working together when you consider what the project aims to achieve? The team itself can make or break the project. If they don't have the right expertise, the project is dead in the water. They also have to believe in the project and want it to succeed.

- Look at the project itself – what are the goals here? What are they setting out to do? Does that make sense or sound like something there would be a market for? The project usually starts with an idea that someone feels will work. Have they done adequate research to ensure that it is as good an idea as they thought?

- What other buzz can you find about the project? What is everyone else saying about it? A newer project might not have generated a lot of buzz yet, but there are many industry experts that monitor new developments and talk about exciting newcomers. It might take a little while to build up the buzz, but if the project is a little older and there is still no buzz, it might be an indication that it is something that the market is not really interested in.

- Has the development team had successes in the past? Has the team delivered in the past? Do they work well together? How many successes and failures have they had? Is it bad luck, or just that the team cannot deliver? Do they have experience in the business world as well?

Homework is the absolute key to getting this right. There is no way that I can stress that enough for you. A lot of people compare ICO investing to having a gold mine. Sure, there is a good chance for a great return with a gold mine, but you have to know where to dig and actually do the hard work to get the gold out.

Legal Issues and ICOs

Most ICOs classify themselves as digital products so that they can get around the strict regulations that are enforced for financial instruments and investments. This is still a grey area, but it is one receiving a lot of attention with government and is set to change.

Take the example of the now defunct BitConnect. SEC investigations into the scheme found that it was primarily a Ponzi scheme and sent out Cease and Desist letters. This was a reasonably popular cryptocurrency, and its value had gone up to just over $300. After the scandal broke, the value plummeted to $32, showing just how volatile the market is. The company then closed the currency down.

Should we feel sorry for the investors? In this case, not really. They apparently did not do their homework because the company never even produced a white paper. This should have sent up a red flag immediately because there was nothing to show that the company had done any research at all.

Anyway, back to the legalities – there are measures being taken worldwide to start regulating these types of investments but, for now, we are in a grey area when it comes to the law. Do, however, expect this to change in future.

At the moment though, the investments do not carry the same kind of protection for the investor that traditional investments do.

Chapter Summary

In this chapter you have learned:

- That an ICO is a way to fund project development or growth for a company.
- That it is more similar to a crowdfunding exercise than to stocks.
- That Ethereum was the first company that used this source of crowdfunding.

- That developers may use static funding or dynamic funding when trying to get their product off the ground and the differences between the two.
- That the market is volatile.
- You could earn a lot of money by being able to get in at ground level.
- You could also lose all your money because the project might fail, or it might be a scam.
- A famous ICO, BitConnect, has recently been outed as a Ponzi scheme and had to shut down operations as a result.
- That it is essential to properly evaluate a project before you decide to buy into it. This means looking at the team, the idea and the history of the project more critically.
- At present, the legalities of these investments are still a bit murky. There is very little regulation of ICOs. However, governments have started to take notice and will be tightening up the laws governing these investments.

In the next chapter, you will learn more about the advantages and disadvantages of ICOs as an investment.

Chapter Three: The Advantages And Disadvantages Of Investing In ICOs

In this chapter, you will learn what the advantages and pitfalls are when it comes to investing in ICOs and also the difference between ICOs and IPOs

People have been quick to jump on the bandwagon when it comes to investing in ICOs. Who can blame them – after all, there has been so much buzz about Bitcoin and its meteoric increase in value that no one wants to miss out on the next big thing.

It's led to a flood of investment in this arena. This, in turn, has led to the influx of new companies hoping to get a piece of that investment money.

There is, however, a difference between not wanting to miss out and being a savvy investor. Let's start by looking at the advantages and disadvantages of investing in ICOs.

Advantages

- They help worthwhile projects get off the ground a lot faster by allowing them to raise funds in a non-traditional way. Getting start-up money in the traditional sphere can be somewhat difficult to accomplish, with conventional investors wanting companies to jump through some serious hoops.

- Investors get to come in at the very best possible price. The initial coin offering is bound to be the lowest price for those tokens and investors can take advantage of this. They have access to investing before the project even starts. This allows for the maximum potential for growth if the company succeeds.

- No bureaucracy to get around. Think of all the red tape you would have to overcome if you were to try and startup a more traditional company. In many cases, companies never make it off the ground because of all of the red tape that they have to wade through. With ICOs, however, the developer and the investor can interact directly. There is no intermediary that must be satisfied first. All the developer needs it a good idea, a well-written white paper, and good marketing. From then on, it is up to the investors to invest or not. Developers can see whether or not there is a good grounding for their product without spending too much money – after all, if the ICO doesn't pan out, it is an indication that the team is doing something wrong.

- At present, there are few regulations governing this sphere, and this makes it easier for both the investor and the developer – though this seems set to change quickly. My best advice here, especially if you are in the United States, is to read up on securities laws. We will go into this in more detail later, but it is better to approach the investment as if it was a security and follow the regulations in this regard as closely as possible.

- They don't tend to follow a typical corporate structure, enabling them to do away with extraneous staff that are not really necessary. So, the startup is able to save money on staffing and use it where it really counts.

Disadvantages

- The same lack of regulation that can be a boon for worthwhile projects also creates a free zone for people out to scam you. Don't fool yourself, there are a lot of scams in the ICO world, and once you have sent them the money, there is little to no chance of recovering it. Fortunately, most scams are pretty easy to recognize when you know what to look for.

- This is speculation at its best. You are putting your money behind an idea that might or might not work. You will know how to look out for scams, and that will protect you a little. That doesn't mean that you won't lose your money. If the idea tanks or the developers are unable to bring it to fruition, your money is pretty much gone because the tokens will lose their value.
- The regulators are coming. Regulation is something that works against the intent of blockchain technology. One of the significant advantages of the blockchain is that there is no central authority to censor or tell it how to run, but in the investment arena, investors do need some form of protection.

Initial Coin Offerings Vs. Initial Public Offerings

If you are looking for a more traditional investment path, Initial Public Offerings (IPOs) are no doubt something you have looked into. On the surface, both investments seem to be the same, but they are very different.

Both are used to raise capital for development or expansion, and ICOs are based on the IPO model, but that's about where the similarities end.

With ICOs, you invest by exchanging tokens for a more established cryptocurrency like Ether or Bitcoin. You are assigned the rights that the company decides to give you. There are no automatically assigned rights.

Unlike with IPOs, you do not automatically become a shareholder and so usually do not have a say in the running of the company. Being a token-holder will not entitle you to have a look at the finances either, so it is a much more hands-off type of investment.

There are cases where ICOs do offer voting rights or allow contributions from investors, but you are more likely to have to pay a premium for these, and these cases are the exception versus the rule.

People buy ICOs because they either believe that the project is a good one and want to show support, or they want to get a good return on their investment. (And, most times, it's a little of both.)

IPOs are also about raising funds, usually to help the company grow more quickly, but here you are buying shares in the business. As a shareholder, you will have some sort of say in how the company is run and are entitled to see the financial statements of the company.

ICOs are part of the free market. This means that they are mostly unregulated. They can get away with selling just an idea. If you invest in them, and the project doesn't take off, you have no legal recourse against them. That's the trade-off for a potentially massive return. It's the same with any investment – the higher the risk, the higher the reward.

With IPOs, on the other hand, there are a lot more regulations in place to protect shareholders. In order to become a publicly listed company, the company must adhere to these rules. This includes releasing annual financial statements that have been independently audited.

Setting up an IPO is a lot more difficult than setting up an ICO, and that is why developers may take advantage and choose an ICO. Having said that, though, more regulations are on the cards, so the gap between IPOs and ICOs is narrowing all the time.

Taxation of the two options is handled a little differently. If you invest in an IPO, profits might be subject to capital gains tax. Technically, the same is true if you invest in an ICO, but presently there is no legislation that deals specifically with cryptocurrencies.

Again, that is something that is bound to change. Uncle Sam and other governments worldwide are actively looking for ways to monitor and tax cryptocurrency exchanges. They also want their piece of the action.

The final difference between the two is that IPOs are forced to follow a more rigid, traditional structure –

investors want to see that there is a CFO, a board of directors, etc. ICOs follow a much less rigid corporate structure, often only sticking to the core staff needed for the project and no one else. This increases the flexibility of the organization and can help to reduce overhead, but it might also work against the ICO if they don't have the right expertise at their disposal.

Chapter Summary

In this chapter you have learned:

- That there are some attractive advantages to ICO investments.
- That these advantages typically stem from the fact that ICOs are more loosely structured, easier to get off the ground and less highly regulated.
- They make it possible for those who need funding to get their idea out to investors in a straightforward manner so that both can benefit.
- ICOs allow investors to invest early on, thereby maximizing the potential return on investment.
- The idea for ICOs is derived from IPOs, but the two are very different from one another.
- Both ICOs and IPOs are used to raise money. Buying into an ICO, however, is not likely to

get you voting rights in the company or access to financial statements.
- The primary difference between ICOs and IPOs is that the latter are a lot more heavily regulated and more efficiently taxed.
- Indications are that ICOs will move closer to the IPO model in terms of regulation and taxation.

In the next chapter, you will learn what makes for a good ICO and what the stages of each project are.

Chapter Four: What Makes For A Great ICO?

In this chapter, you will learn what a good ICO is made of and what stages of the project are the best times to invest.

You picked up this book for a reason – maybe you have heard some incredible ICO success stories, where investors ended up making a pile of money. Where investors quadrupled their money in next to no time at all. Who here hasn't seen an article about Bitcoin billionaires. ICOs are the hot and happening place to invest now.

The problem is that most investors don't understand how things work, or that there are many failures interspersed amongst the success stories. The ICOs that fail don't make headlines, but there are many of them out there.

In 2017, according to Bitcoin Market Journal, 35% of ICOs opened in 2017 did not report their funding statistics. While there might be several other figures at play, this is most likely an indication that they just did not meet their funding targets and did not want to advertise the fact.

What Makes An ICO Successful?

To be considered successful, an ICO must raise at least 75% of its funding target by selling its tokens. If, for example, the company decided to issue 100 000 tokens and sold 76 000 of these, the ICO would be considered successful. If they sold 72 000, however, they would not.

If the ICO does not bring in enough money, the chances of the company failing further down the line increase significantly. A lack of working capital is something that causes many startups to fail – they cannot devote the resources to furthering their idea or supporting the business.

While an ICO-based company does not have a traditional structure, it is, in essence, a startup and so prone to the same kinds of issues that startups could have problems with.

Many ICOs will never reach their target funding and so are less likely to complete successfully, and this is something that you need to be aware of. Trends indicate that investors are becoming more discerning when it comes to ICO investing, opting more for the lower risk options than ones that could fail.

It seems that your typical investor's appetite for risk is lowering, meaning that ICOs have to do a lot more work to convince a potential investor to invest in the current climate.

How Do I Know Which ICOs Are Lower Risk?

Doing proper research is key to understanding which ICOs have a better chance of succeeding. That means reading the white paper and researching the idea more.

There are a lot to wade through, though and, if you don't have time to read through pages and pages of white papers, knowing what stage the product that the ICO is producing is in can be a useful way to cut down your options. You will know instantly which to put on the slush pile because they don't match your appetite for risk.

The Four Stages

There are four stages of product development that you will see when looking into ICOs:

1. **The Idea Stage**: During this phase, all you have to go on is an idea. No one has yet put any thought into the direction development might take or done a lot of market research. The team may or may not have been put together yet. At this stage, the tokens are likely to be at their

least expensive, but the chances of it failing are at the highest. ICOs in this stage are, at best, a risky investment or, at worst, a con job. If you invest at this stage, you must be prepared to lose your whole investment. I am not saying that you should never invest in an ICO at this stage, but you should only do so when you are more experienced. This is not a good investment for a beginner to make.

2. **The White Paper Stage**: This is when the idea has moved out of the conception phase and a lot more thought and effort has been put into it. In a later chapter, we will look for what constitutes a good white paper. At this stage, you have more than a simple idea, but you don't have a working product yet, so there is still some risk involved. If they cannot solve the problem in the way they aim to, there will be no return on your investment. This is the stage that most ICOs you encounter will be at. You need to verify then that what they have said in their white paper is accurate.

3. **The Proven Developer Stage**: This is where the developer or company have already created products. It may not be exactly the same as what they are currently planning to work on, but it has a higher chance of success because the team has proven that they can do something similar. An example of this would be

icon omni. Let's say, for example; you have a developer that has previously released photo editing software that is in high demand. Maybe now they have decided to add a scanning app. It's not exactly the same thing, but the developer gets some leeway because of their proven ability. Investing at this stage would be a little more expensive, but the chances of success are also much higher.

4. **The Prototype Stage**: This would be the most expensive time to invest, but it is also the time when the chances of success are highest. There is a working model of the product that can be checked and tested. You know the product works and how it works. The best example of this is Ethereum itself. The developers built the software first and tested it before having an ICO. This is the lowest risk option because there is no question about whether or not the project is possible. All that needs to happen here is that it is marketed correctly.

You need to select the option that suits your investment profile the best. Are you okay with a high-risk investment or do you want something that has a better chance of success? What about spreading the risk a little?

It is a good idea in any investment portfolio to consider what your short-term and long-term goals are. If you are retiring in two years' time, is it a good idea to sink all your savings into a cryptocurrency investment? No, because if you lose it all, you have very little time to recover from the loss.

When deciding whether or not to invest, a good way to think of it is to determine when you will need the money. ICO investments are usually medium to long-term investments, depending on how quickly the project takes off.

My advice, use money that you won't need for at least the next two years here and never use money that you cannot afford to lose.

Chapter Summary

In this chapter you have learned:

- That many ICOs will fail. They are startup companies and so prone to the same kinds of issues.
- That a successful ICO is one that brings in at least three-quarters of the expected amount. Capital is extremely important when it comes to product development.
- That there are four stages when it comes to ICO investing.
- The highest risk of failure is during the Idea Stage before much research has been done.

- The highest chance of success is when a working prototype is available for testing. So, after all the development work has been completed.

In the next chapter, you will learn how you can recognize an ICO scam and protect yourself from investing in one.

Chapter Five: What Do ICO Scams Look Like?

In this chapter, you will learn about the red flags when it comes to ICO scams and how you can minimize your chances of being involved in them.

ICOs make for an interesting investment opportunity. Not many people understand them well, and there has been a lot of buzz about them lately. Throw in that there is very little regulation with these investments, and you have the perfect recipe for con artists to have a field day.

If you are going to start investing in this market, you need to be on your guard – there are ICOs out there that are wonderful, and there are those that are scams. You can never be 100% certain that you are not going to get caught, but the tips we go through below will help reduce the risks for you.

For the most part, view everything you are told with a healthy skepticism. Verify the information you are given and if you cannot, move along.

If You See These, Run

- **The ICO is shrouded in secrecy**: They don't want you to know who owns it, you cannot trace the domain name, and you cannot access the smart contracts to see how they are set up. It's amazing how many people today will put up with anonymity online when they wouldn't live in real life. If a stranger on the street came to you and offered to double your money, you would wonder what the catch was. You probably wouldn't do it. Why take the same chance online? By the same token, if you were going to invest in a startup in the real world, you would want to read through the contract first, wouldn't you? Legitimate companies want you to be completely comfortable with investing with them. They will provide the information you require. Scam artists will only give you what you want up to a certain point. They don't want you to understand too much because they don't want you getting wise to the scam.

- **A hard-sell or company desperate to push you to invest**: You know the kind of salesperson I am talking about. The type that corners you in the department store and doesn't let go. They are charming, and you may even like them at first, but it quickly becomes apparent that they want you to buy something and that they don't intend to take no for an answer. If this happens with an ICO get out of it now. You don't want to be pressured into deciding in a hurry. You need to be left to do your own research, and a legitimate company will understand that. If the ICO is closing in twenty minutes, look for something else – there is not enough time to accurately assess that one.
- **Not Verifiable on LinkedIn**: Okay, now I realize that many business people don't maintain their LinkedIn profiles but an ICO that is serious about investors will. Check out the names of those that are said to be involved and check their profiles as well. Do they reference the project at all? Is there a company page for it? It is highly unusual for nothing to check out. Where are the team members based? What sometimes happens is that scam artists use the profiles of reputable-looking people and claim them as team members. So, if you see what looks like discrepancies between the LinkedIn profile and the team profile, contact

the team member on LinkedIn and raise the issue. If it is a genuine error, you will find out quite quickly. If it is a scam, you will know, and you will have warned the person whose reputation is at risk as well.

- **Is the company registered anywhere**? If so, the country it is registered in could give an indication of how good the investment is. For example, the laws in Singapore regarding ICOs are more flexible. In the United States and Europe, countries are starting to crack down. That's not to say that all ICOs registered in more lax countries are problematic, but you do have to wonder why they registered somewhere other than the country they are based in. Fraudsters will often use accounts found in places like the Cayman Islands. It just does not bode well for the longevity of the company when they try to sidestep regulations in the country that they are based in. What happens in two or three years' time? Is there even going to still be a company?
- **Anonymous domain registration**: Try running a search on a site like WhoIs to see if you can find out who the owners of the site are. If the site owner is private in this case, you have to wonder why. Perhaps the site owner values their privacy, and that is understandable; but when it comes to a real ICO, surely, they want

every opportunity to reassure their potential investors that they are for real and to leave open every possible contact opportunity.

- **Where do the funds go?** There are ICOs out there that promise to return money to investors if they don't reach their targets. Legitimate companies will have you put the money into an escrow account that is usually administered by an independent third party. It makes good business sense – that way, nothing can come and bite them in the butt later because everything has been handled in an above-the-board manner. Companies that don't do this are more likely to want to take the money and run.

- **How transparent is the company about its processes?** Does it allow you to have a look at the data in progress? Now, yes, companies will want to keep their proprietary data under wraps, but there should be some element that you can have a look at if you want to. Something like the smart contract setup should not betray any proprietary secrets but still afford you the opportunity to see how they work. Did they think it out logically and well? Is it well-written or cobbled together? How will you know that progress is made if you don't get the odd look under the hood?

- **There is no white paper**: This should instantly quell any desire to invest in the company. There has been no thought given to whether or not the product is one that is useful and how to go about bringing it to fruition. It is unlikely that there has been any market research done beyond tossing some ideas to friends and family, or perhaps a teammate at work. We will go through what elements a great white paper should have in a later chapter but, for now, no white paper means that the company is sloppy at best, or pulling a scam at worst.

- **Is it all too easy**? This is the hallmark of a scam. Everything comes a little too easily. They have a project that looks good on paper and that they know will be brilliant. There are no obstacles in the way, and everything is smooth sailing. There are hiccups along the road for any business, and someone who tries to convince you otherwise is probably trying to scam you. If their solution is so perfect and so easy to bring into being, why has no one else done it yet?

- **Finally, what does your gut say**? Do you get the feeling that it's all a little too good to be true? Then it most likely is. Listen to your gut and get out of there. Don't let greed make you act on poor investment advice. It's the oldest con trick in the book – appeal to someone's sense of greed, and you can usually get them to believe what you like. Never believe anything you are told in this sphere and don't trust what the team says without verifying it.

Chapter Summary

In this chapter you have learned:

- Anonymity when it comes to who is in charge of an ICO is usually a bad sign.
- You cannot take anything that you are told at face value – don't trust anything and verify everything yourself.
- Don't let anyone push you or rush you into making a decision. Scammers often want you to commit fast before you have a chance to check things out or change your mind.
- The more secretive the company is, the more likely it is that it is a scam.
- Con artists will often promise to pay the money back if they don't raise enough. Don't let this lull you into a false sense of security. Make sure that the money is paid into a suitable escrow account so that refunds are at the discretion of an independent third party.
- No white paper should mean that your money should stay in your wallet. A good white paper is a roadmap to success – why wouldn't a company invest in one?

- If there are no problems and the process is so easy, someone else would have surely come up with the same idea before now. If the team does not acknowledge that there might be problems along the way, they are either delusional or scamming you.
- Listen to your intuition. If it seems to be too good to be true, walk away. Don't let the promise of easy money override your good sense.

In the next chapter, you will learn what a good white paper should include.

Chapter six: How Do I Know That The White paper Is Any Good?

In this chapter, you will learn how to tell the difference between an excellent white paper and a bad one.

Why have I been harping on about the white paper? Simply put, a white paper is similar to a business plan. It shows you step by step what the developers are planning to do and how well it is written and thought out gives an indication of how much planning has gone into making this idea a reality.

The white paper can make or break a company. If the white paper is vague or glosses over potential issues without addressing them adequately, it is an indication that the writer does not know what is going on and is probably unsure of how to continue.

A white paper that has been written on the fly and that contains typos or looks like it has been rushed through is also a bad sign. This is often the only chance that the business has to impress potential investors. If they cannot be bothered to make an effort here, how diligent will they be when it comes to overcoming problems in development or creating a product that is glitch-free?

Are they serious about the company at all? How diligent have they been in their research if they let typos slip through the cracks? Why haven't they deemed it necessary to hire someone to write the paper for them? If they don't want to invest the time and effort in producing a professional white paper, why would you want to invest with them at all?

An excellent white paper, on the other hand, addresses all the technical and commercial aspects of the project. It is thoughtfully written, based on fact, not supposition and gives you all the information that you need to know. It deals with how the product will be developed, marketed and sold and also deals with issues that might be encountered.

It should tell the investor what the unique value proposition for this product is and how they will stand out from the competition. Why this product, made this way and at this time? Why will it be a success and, most importantly, why will it work in the market as it stands?

What A Good White Paper Should Contain

- **An excellent executive summary**: Good white papers tend to be longer documents. They are not documents that you dive into when you have a few minutes to spare. The executive summary will go over the main points covered in a very succinct form. It's there to whet your appetite and to encourage you to read further. Now, if this is the first ICO white paper you are looking at, you will no doubt have set aside some time to read it. The executive summary won't seem quite as important initially, but you have to also consider other investors. You don't want to be the only one investing. Is the summary compelling? Does it make you want to read more about the project or take action? Would it stand out if there were ten other white papers in front of you as well? A well-written executive summary should hook the reader and make them want to read the rest of the document.

- **A thorough description of the problem**: What problem will this product help to solve? Is it a compelling problem? Is it something that most people would be looking for a solution for? When reading this, keep your thinking cap on. Focus on the issue itself and how much of a problem it is.

- **The solution**: How is the product going to solve the problem? How are people dealing with this issue at the moment? How much will you need to charge and is that something that they'd be willing to pay? Would they be willing to spend money on that solution or could they get by as they are now? Are there other ways to get around the problem or better solutions for the problem? When it comes to that, what other things do they have to consider when buying this solution? For example, a budgeting app with all the bells and whistles might be a nice to have and can make it easier to manage expenses. However, a notebook and pen, or an Excel spreadsheet could do the same for a lot less money. Which would be easier for the potential client? What are they used to doing now? Maybe solving this problem is not as high on their list of priorities.
- **The product and cycle**: What is the product that they are proposing? What different milestones are they putting in place for the development of this product? How will they know if things are on track or not? How advanced is the development of the product? Does it require new technology to make it work or are the component parts available already? Something that is brand new and starting from scratch is bound to take a longer time to

develop and require more money to produce, than something where the component parts are already available. That's not to say that you shouldn't invest because it will take time, but the company must explain this to you upfront.

- **The team**: Who is doing what? Who are the key players and what are their roles? Why are they the best people for the job? What are their credentials or experience? What do they bring to the table and how will they assist in the success of the company? Why are they passionate about this particular project?
- **The market and competition**: What market will they be working in? Who will they sell to? How big is the market? What products are out there already? Who is the competition – both direct and indirect - and what are they offering?
- **The token market**: What are you going to be able to do with the tokens outside of the company? Will you be able to buy, sell or trade them? If the company goes bust, is there another application for the tokens?
- **How the proceeds are going to be used**: The company should have worked out some sort of budget and so should be able to lay out how they will use the funds that they are raising to develop the product. Where are they spending most of the money? Are they paying designers, paying for legal costs, marketing, etc.? Do they

have a clear idea of what expenses there are? Have they taken most of the potential costs into account? This section should quite detailed if the company has done their research.

- **Terms and conditions**: If you buy a token, what are your rights? Do you have voting rights at all? Has there already been a presale where investors have been able to purchase tokens at a lower value? (This could affect the overall value of your tokens.) How many tokens are to be issued? This is something that has a serious effect on the value of the tokens going forward. Take Bitcoin, for example. The number of Bitcoins is finite, once 21 million have been issued, no new Bitcoins will be available. Around about three-quarters of this figure have already been mined, and that is why people have been losing their minds when it comes to Bitcoin investments. They are seen as a commodity that is getting rarer by the day. On the other hand, if Bitcoins were limitless in supply, they would devalue very quickly because they would flood the market.

- **The intrinsic value**: Some coins are merely cryptocurrency that can be bought, sold and traded. Some coins have a more practical function in that they allow you to pay for using the product or services from the company. What will your coins enable you to do? Ether, for example, was not explicitly developed as a cryptocurrency but rather as a way for developers and users of the Ethereum network to pay for services used. So, if you want to set up a smart contract, for example, you need to pay in Ether. You need to know exactly what it is that you are buying.

Chapter Summary

In this chapter you have learned:

- That an excellent white paper is detailed and shows the amount of thought that the developers have put into the project.
- A white paper is similar in nature to a business plan and should give you all the information you need with regards the team and the plan that they are going to follow to develop, market and sell the product.
- The white paper is the company's best chance of getting investors interested. If they do a poor job of it, they are not likely to reach their funding goals.
- If the white paper does not impress you, it is not likely to impress others either. The team should spend time on perfecting the white paper before releasing it because it gives a clear

signal about how seriously the project is being taken.

In the next chapter, you will learn about how to evaluate the team behind the ICO.

Chapter Seven: It's All About Teamwork

In this chapter, you will learn why the team behind the ICO is so essential and how to make sure that the team that you are presented with are the right people for the job.

Starting and managing any company is difficult. This is especially true when it comes to ICOs. You have to have the right team for the job, a team that has the necessary skills and that is able to work well with one another. Without experience and cohesion, the team starts out at a disadvantage.

How To Get More Information About The Team

Start out by looking at the ICO's website and in the white paper for details about the team. If they have no details in either place, look for a different ICO to invest in. If they don't have enough details, you can ask the company to provide them. Most businesses will be more than happy to comply with reasonable requests like this one.

Is The Team Any Good?

Now you need to prepare yourself to do a little legwork. It is essential to properly evaluate the team and make sure that they can deliver on their promises. It doesn't matter how wonderful the idea is if it is poorly executed it will not succeed. In fact, it may just serve as inspiration for a competitor who has the team to execute a better version, leaving your investment in the dust.

To evaluate the team, you must:

- **Google each of the team members**: Is there information about them, their experience and background that you can draw from? Do a quick experiment and Google your name. There is a surprising amount of information that you can find this way. If you cannot find any info on the team members, this should be a red flag. We live a lot of our world online. Someone might not have a Facebook profile, but they are bound to be on some kind of social media or linked to some sort of project somewhere.
- **Check on LinkedIn**: Do their profiles on LinkedIn match what you have been told? What other work experiences do they have? Have they been published? Do they look like the photos displayed on LinkedIn and other social media? Are they who they claim to be?

- **What kind of reputation do they have?** Someone who strikes out on their own to start an ICO is risking their reputation if things go wrong. If they have a good reputation already, they are less likely to risk ruining it by getting involved with a dodgy project. That's no guarantee that the project is a good one, but it should help the case for the project.
- **What is their background?** What credentials and practical experience do they have that actually relates to what the ICO needs? Think about what you would be looking for if you had to set up your own team for this project. You would want people with some recent experience in the field. Think of it this way, would you go and look at a bunch of accountants if you wanted to start a professional baseball team? No, you would look for players. The same applies here, some experience in the field is required for at least a few of the team members. Considering the nature of this market, it is also crucial that they are up to date with their skills and experience. Someone who got a degree in computer science a decade ago and has not kept up with advances in the field is not going to have the skills to work on the Ethereum network, for example.
- **Their team history**: Have they worked with one another before? How will they work as a

team together? Generally speaking, it is better to have a team whose members have had some work experience with one another. That way each member knows what to expect from the others, and there is less chance of falling out over small misunderstandings. In a stressful environment, you need to be able to work with the members of your team as it is quite common for nerves to become frayed. You don't want one of the team members to walk out when the project is nearing completion.

- **Do they have experience with blockchain?** In this game, saying something like, "We'll get the funding and then find the talent" can be fatal. The blockchain is something that is still very new, and there are only a certain number of experts out there. The team should include at least one member who understands the workings of blockchain technology and has some experience working with it.

- **Are the advisors credible and do they have input?** Check the list of advisors and see how much influence they actually have. There is a big difference between having an advisor looking over the initial plan once and give pointers and someone who is actually on board and helping to make the project a success by providing advice on a more regular basis. Both people would be called advisors, but the latter has a much more hands-on role.

Chapter Summary

In this chapter you have learned:

- That good teamwork is essential to the success of the project.
- That you need to vet the team working on the ICO properly by checking online sources and confirming that what they have claimed is true.
- Experience in the field is both an asset and essential to success.
- That the advisor's ongoing role is also essential.

In the next chapter, you will learn about evaluating the market projections and also how to check whether or not the ICO's competitor analyses are accurate.

Chapter Eight: How To Evaluate The ICO's Market Projections And Competitor Analyses

In this chapter, you will learn how you can verify whether the ICO's market projections and competitor analyses are realistic or not.

So, you think they have a good idea, and they have set up a good team. Now we need to go a step further and make sure that there actually is a market for what they plan to sell. Remember that the value of a product is only ever as much as someone is willing to pay for it.

In his lifetime, Vincent Van Gogh was penniless. He battled to give his art away, and couldn't make a good living from it. Nowadays it is very different. His work sells for millions, but it illustrates my point perfectly.

You need to make sure not only that there is a market for the product, but also that there is enough of a market to make it profitable. The ICO should have done some good market research, but you need to understand how to evaluate it and come up with your own conclusions to make an informed decision.

Let's start off with some basic terminology that you are likely to encounter.

Total Addressable Market (TAM)

This is the total number of people that the ICO could possibly sell to. Let's say they are making a budgeting dapp. The TAM, in this case, would be all the people in the world who use their cellphones to help them budget, regardless of location or demographics. It would be anyone that might possibly be interested in using the dapp.

Serviceable Available Market (SAM)

The TAM would give quite a large number, but it is not a highly accurate reflection of the actual situation. While there may be billions that the app would be of interest to, you also have to account for differences such as geographical location, language, etc. The ICO would not, for example, be able to sell the dapp in North Korea.

They might have to limit the market to people who could speak English, for example, and maybe narrow it further to those who use US dollars as their currency. The ICO will target people according to their own criteria to make marketing efforts more focused and productive.

Serviceable Obtainable Market (SOM)

Now we are getting somewhere. This is the figure that you should pay the most attention to because it refers to the market share that the company thinks it can gain. So, the total number of people who will actually buy the dapp.

Here you need to watch out for companies who overinflate these numbers. A market share of 10% to 15% is reasonable but watch out for companies that project a considerable market share, like 50% or something similar. Reaching this kind of market penetration takes a long time and is not so easily done. This is more usually an indication that either they are overoptimistic, that they haven't done their research correctly or that they are trying to pull a scam.

Compound Annual Growth Rate (CAGR)

This is another important figure. The compound annual growth rate is an average taken over a few years of the company's actual growth rate or projected growth rate. Again, this figure is important because it can be an indicator of how your returns may be expected to grow.

You do need to watch out for over-inflated figures here as well. A 10%-15% or even 20% growth may not seem as good as a 50% CAGR, but it is a lot more realistic. Achieving high growth figures is also something that is not so easily accomplished, especially since the market changes and new entrants or global circumstances may shake up the game.

Ask yourself whether or not the projections make sense in light of current economic trends and factors.

How Do I Apply This New Knowledge?

Now that you understand the terminology have a look at the data that the company has provided. How detailed is it? How deeply have they drilled into the data? For example, have they divided the SOM up into different demographics or have they lumped it all together?

Different market sectors mean that different approaches are required. This makes segmenting the market correctly an essential task and something that a serious ICO would take into consideration. If they are lumping all the sectors together, their marketing efforts are bound to be less focused and less efficient.

Have a look at their figures. Do the statistics seem credible and logical? Let's go back to our budget dapp as an example. How many people in the target market are likely to buy it? Bearing in mind that users will need to be convinced to try it and replace whatever system they were using before, is a projection of 50% market share realistic?

Work through each of the figures and evaluate them individually to see whether or not they make sense. If they don't, it is time to move onto a different ICO.

If they do, it is time to check how credible the sources for the information are and to see if you can validate the information on your own. Be wary of white papers that don't list the sources for their information. Remember the golden rule – a good team will want to give investors every reason to invest. This means finding credible and verifiable sources of data and linking to these sources.

If they haven't listed the sources, why haven't they? Is it because they have made the statistics up? Is it because they have used less-than-reliable sources? If the sources are credible, the company has more to gain from listing them than not.

With any data analysis, there will also be some underlying assumptions that have to be made. Find out what these assumptions were in this case – the white paper should also reference these clearly.

Check The Market Data

It is natural for a company to skew market data by focusing only on the positives. Technically, they are not doing anything wrong by doing this, but you really are not going to get the whole picture this way either. It's homework time again – you need to see whether or not you can confirm that the data presented is accurate.

You can do that by Googling a search term such as "Cellphone market size analyses California." If you cannot find anything quite that specific, you can try looking for statistics regarding the general market that is being targeted.

From that information, you can draw up the TAM, SOM, and SAM for yourself and see how closely it matches the company's figures.

Look for the average CAGR for the industry in general and for the company, if applicable to see what potential there is for growth in future.

Analyzing the Competitive Analysis

Every well-thought-out white paper needs to have a competitive analysis. That is where the company evaluates the competition in the market, both direct and indirect.

What competitors are out there? Are there people doing the same thing the ICO plans to do? If so, what is the company's unique value proposition? Why should people choose them over their competitor? Research into the size of the market goes hand in hand with the competitive analyses. Without a proper competitive analysis, a company could make a number of costly mistakes.

Be wary of the company if there is no competitive analysis, or they say that they have no competitors at all. This is usually an indication that they have not done their homework correctly. It is highly unlikely that they have come up with a problem that no one else has ever tried to solve.

If they do claim that they have no competitors, you also have to wonder why that is. If this is such a pressing problem, why are more companies not trying to solve it? It could be that there is not a big enough market, or it could be that people have found a way around the problem. Maybe it isn't important enough to get them to spend money on a solution.

Whichever way you look at it, the fact that there are no competitors is probably a bad sign.

The competitive analysis should address the following:

- **What companies have come up with a solution to the problem and what have they done?** What can this company do better? A company can differentiate itself by offering better features, a better prize or better geographical coverage. If they are just coming up with the same solution again, they are bound to be seen as following the crowd rather than as innovators.

- **What barriers to entry are there?** When the new company wants to enter the market, they want as few barriers to entry as possible. However, they also want it to be difficult for others to follow suit or they will lose market share pretty fast. Check the barriers to entry for the market the ICO is considering. How long will they have the technical advantage for?
- **Are there any regulations to consider?** Take the example of BitConnect, for example. Initially, they were on to a pretty good thing. However, once the SEC got involved, they were forced to shut down. Is the company you are considering skating on thin ice when it comes to tighter regulations? If so, they are not a good investment.

Going through the information like this is time-consuming, but it is worth putting in the effort. The more you want to invest, the more diligent you need to be. There are sites that make the process a little easier, so if you are pressed for time, you can also check out how the ICO rates on the following sites:

- smithandcrown.com
- ICOrating.com

One last word for this chapter – don't believe anything you are told in the white paper until you have been able to verify it independently.

Chapter Summary

In this chapter you have learned:

- What common industry terms mean and how to interpret them.
- How to carefully evaluate the data contained in market reports and market analyses.
- How to verify this data externally.
- How to come up with your own conclusions.

In the next chapter, you will learn more about evaluating the business model and how this affects token sales.

Chapter Nine: Evaluating The Business Model

In this chapter, you will learn how to find out whether or not the ICO is following a good business model, what means they might use when it comes to token sales and how to see what is happening to the money that you invest.

The Business Model

You need to start out by asking the right questions when it comes to the business model that the ICO has presented. Here's what you need to know:

- **What is the underlying system, and does it make sense here?** Does it make sense for the company to want an extensive network or are they just looking for a way to access funding? For example, the local undertaker would not really need a wide network of people from other cities, would they? If the underlying system does not make sense for the business, it is time to look at another ICO.

- **Is a decentralized network appropriate?** Will moving the company onto the blockchain network have real benefits for the company or will it just be a waste of time?
- **Why have they got tokens?** How will the tokens be used? Is there a specific purpose within the company or are they purely speculative? Does the business model actually require them to sell tokens? While most companies do look for a cash injection from time to time, you need to know why they are doing so now. Do they plan to expand (Usually good for the investor) or do they need money because they are battling? If they haven't laid out what they plan to use the investment money for, be very wary.
- **What economic model do they follow?** This is key because it tells you how they intend to create value for the investors. Is this project going to be a one-hit wonder or do they plan to expand it if successful?
- **Is there any outside application for the token?** If the project goes bust, will there be any other ways to use the token? Can it be used

with other products within the company, or with partners?

The Objectives Of A Token Sale

A token sale could be held for a number of different reasons – sure, the company wants to raise money, but how they are handling the sale will tell you a lot about what those reasons are.

- **To reach a certain minimum in sales**: This is common and involves the team creating a target in sales based on how much money they need to operate. It shows that they have done some homework and are not just trying to raise as much as possible – when they hit that minimum, they are likely to stop issuing coins. It pays to remember that the coins can become a commodity in themselves, and the team members will probably also get some. If they are serious about the business, they will want to sell just enough to meet their needs but not so much that they flood the market.
- **Placing a cap on the amount raised**: So, the company will accept sales figures below this but will stop selling the token when they have raised as much money as they need.
- **Issue a set number of tokens**: This is essentially what Bitcoin did – they are not going to issue more Bitcoins once 21 million have

been issued. The benefit for the investor is that the scarcer the commodity is, the more the token will become worth if the company takes off.

- **They want wide-scale adoption**: This means that they are going to sell as many tokens to as many people as possible. The company might do something like this if their business model requires them to have an extensive network. Something like Ethereum, for example. Watch out here though if you cannot find a good business reason for this kind of scaling. It could also indicate a scam.
- **They could sell the tokens for their market value**: Here they are looking for investors and are willing to roll the dice that they will get enough investors.
- **They could ensure that every buyer gets some tokens**: This might mean issuing as many tokens as were bought instead of limiting the supply up front.
- **They could make sure that every buyer gets some percentage of the tokens issued**: This works well where they want to limit supply but ensure that all the buyers do get something.

Companies will need to decide which objectives suit them best before the sale. There is no way that any company can run with all these objectives at once.

The Types Of Token Sales

The objectives that the company has will determine what type of token sale they offer. There are a lot of different models to choose from, so here we will be concentrating on the top five most common ones.

Capped Sales – First Come First Served

This will usually mean that a set number of tokens is issued. The prices of each token will be the same and will only change once all the tokens have been sold. They could, instead, place a cap on the overall value of sales but the outcome will be the same – when the goal is reached, no more tokens will be issued. Team members will be issued tokens in pre-determined quantities.

Uncapped Sales

In this case, the company will run the sale over a set period of time and tokens will be issued without any limits. So, the company could sell 100 tokens, or they could sell 100 000 tokens. This option allows the buyer to buy any amount they wish. Team members receive a set number of tokens in this case as well.

Capped Auction

This works slightly differently. Buyers will bid on tokens. The bids will determine the value of the token. The tokens will be sold until a particular cash value has been raised and so the numbers of tokens issued will change. Team members will receive a variable number of tokens, based on how many have been sold.

Uncapped Auction

This is just like the option above except that there are no limits in terms of cash raised. The number of tokens, however, will be limited. The prices per token will vary depending on the bid amounts. The team members will receive a percentage of the overall number of tokens.

Capped And Then Redistributed

This is another auction, but this time the buyers bid on the amount that they would like to pay. The distribution of tokens will depend on how many were sold, and which prices were most favorable. With this kind of auction, you might see the company refunding some of the investors whose bids they didn't want to accept.

Use of Proceeds

Now that we understand the basics of how the sale will work, we need to look at one of the most important aspects to look at – how the money you pay for tokens will be used by the company.

A legitimate and forward-thinking company will have created a budget and will know exactly what their financial goals are. They will have a plan on how they are going to spend that money and should be willing to share that plan with you.

It's the same as any startup company – if they want funding, they have to prove to potential investors what they are planning to do with the money. It is also something that the SEC would be very interested in, so it is important that the ICO has a solid plan.

They should have milestones in place for each stage of the process. Ideally, you want a breakdown along the lines of:

Section To Spend Money In	Percentage To Use
Product Development	50%
Marketing	25%
Legal Costs	10%
Operations Costs	10%
Reserves	5%

You want an ICO where the focus is mainly on development. Without adequate resources dedicated to developing a great product, the process will be delayed. Look at it this way, the sooner the product is produced, the sooner you can start getting a return on your investment.

If the company lays out its plans in this manner in the white paper, then it comes very close to being a contractual obligation. If you wanted to sue at a later stage on the grounds that they misrepresented the investment, you would have a reasonable case.

If the white paper makes no mention of how the funds will be used, or says something along the lines of, "We decide how they are used" it is time to move on.

Valuation Of The ICO

Here is where things become a bit tougher – you don't have access to the more traditional means of checking how the business is doing, like Price over Earnings or Earnings per Share. You also are not likely to have access to industry information on that particular ICO so that you can establish whether or not the token price is overvalued.

Valuing companies operating in the crypto sphere requires a new approach altogether. Here are some points that can help you with that.

Functional Value

This means what the value of the token is. What is it used for? For example, Bitcoin can be used instead of fiat currency. Ethers are another example because you need them to pay for using the Ethereum network when setting up smart contracts or creating dapps. All new tokens of this type issued should have some specific, practical purpose.

Speculative Value

As an investor, this is more the kind of thing that you would be interested in. This value is based on the amount you can earn by trading the coin. Coins with a speculative rather than functional value are designed specifically for fundraising and can be used to help further development. One caveat here, though, if the investment is purely speculative, SEC regulations are going to apply.

How Do I Know If A Token Is Worth Buying?

You can start out by trying to see what the buzz about it is. Do there seem to a lot of investors? Does the business model seem sound and make sense? While we cannot use the traditional ways of assessing a business, we have other ways to do so.

- **Market Size**: The market size is something that is relatively simple to calculate, and it can be used as an indication of whether or not the product is going to sell. It's problematic when used on its own because getting a completely accurate figure is difficult.
- **Discounted Value**: This method is closest to traditional methods of evaluation. Again, this is simple to work out but should not be used on its own. This is because it might be tough to find accurate inputs and you will need to make some basic assumptions. You will need to estimate things like estimated return, and this can be difficult.

What Challenges Are There In Valuing ICOs?

- Little or no project history.
- Projections are difficult to do with great accuracy because success rates are so low.
- The project itself could be solid and well-thought out but dips in the crypto markets could impact negatively on the project.
- These projects are designed around a particular platform, like Ethereum. This can be problematic if the platform is hacked or if it fails in some other way.

Know Your Rights

What rights investors are offered can have a significant impact on how much investment there is. It must always be remembered that shareholders and token holders have very different rights. In this section, we will run through what the most commonly held investor rights are. You should see the rights being offered by checking the terms and conditions or by reading the white paper.

- **Payment rights**: This means that the tokens are going to enable you to pay for the use of the product. What is good about this is that it gives you a very clear indication of what your rights are. The downside is that it will lead to founding of many other cryptocurrencies as each company issues its own tokens and that increases the volatility of the market and gives investors too many choices.
- **Access rights**: This is the one most commonly issued, and it does exactly what it says it does, allows you access to the platform. This is a good way for the company to raise money, but it is not such a good deal for the investor. How many people will pay just to look behind the curtain?
- **Profit Share**: This is the closest that you will get to a traditional stock market investment. On the upside, the potential return on investment is higher. On the downside, these kinds of

agreements do fall under the jurisdiction of the SEC.

- **Contribution**: This enables you to contribute to the success of the project. It could be in maintaining the network, or some similar function. The problem here is that you might end up with one person controlling specific function. This defeats the whole object of decentralizing the project.
- **Block Creation**: You will be able to secure the network through the creation of blocks. Instead of having to solve complex equations to unlock blocks, you are effectively betting your tokens that the block will be solved. This is known as proof of stake – the people with the highest stakes have more chance of unlocking new tokens. The problem here is that not everyone will want to do this.
- **Governance**: This can be a good thing or a bad thing. It is good because the investors have some say in the direction that the company is moving in and may be able to make a useful contribution. It is bad because there could end up being too many opinions issued and this could stall development.

Chapter Summary

In this chapter you have learned:

- How to start evaluating the business model the ICO uses.
- Why the business might be having a token sale and what types of token sales there are.
- Why it is important to know what the money will be used for.
- How to go about valuing the ICO and figuring out if the token is worth investing in.
- What your rights are as an investor.
- What the challenges are when it comes to valuing ICOs.

In the next chapter, you will learn a little bit about the legal standing of ICOs and when you need to exercise caution.

Chapter Ten: Keep A Legal Eye On Things

In this chapter, you will learn why you need to make sure that the ICO is acting in terms of the law or not.

In the beginning, when ICOs were first developed, they were completely unregulated. This was a major win for the companies because it meant that they did not have to comply with the strict rules that govern securities. In the United States, it was easier to market the investment as a digital product and so side step the SEC.

Things are changing and changing very fast. If you are thinking about investing in a token, make sure that you keep your nose clean. Apply the Harvey Test to see whether or the token might be classified as a security. Ask the following:

- Is money being invested?
- Is it a common enterprise?

- Have they created the expectation that you will make a profit?
- Is most of the work going to be done by others?

If your answers to most of these questions are, "Yes," this could be classified as a security in the United States, so you need to proceed with caution. Have they hired the correct investment advisors, are they complying with SEC regulations? If not, and the SEC investigates them, you stand to lose your investment and might even be facing time in court as well.

The time for ICOs to be able to skate by is fast coming to an end. The SEC is currently investigating ICOs and will continue to do so to check whether or not they are selling securities. This may be bad news for the ICOs, but it is all done to protect investors.

Be extremely careful if you come across a company that claims that their offering is exempt. There are a lot of terms and conditions that apply here, and you need to be an accredited investor in order to take up such an offer. Don't get caught out.

Outside Of The United States

The actual regulations that will apply will depend on where the investment is based and the country that you are based in. So far, it appears that the United States has taken the toughest stance when it comes to ICOs, but other countries do seem to be following suit as well.

One thing is certain – more regulation is coming, and the situation is very fluid. It is important to keep up with regulatory matters so that you can ensure that you are always acting legally and that the company you are investing in is doing the same.

Chapter Summary

In this chapter you have learned:

- The rules regarding ICOs are changing rapidly.
- In the United States, the SEC is cracking down on ICOs.
- The regulations governing the ICOs internationally are different from one country to the next.

In the next chapter, you will learn more about the technical aspects of an ICO so that you are better able to evaluate them.

Chapter Eleven: Technical Aspects Of Investing

In this chapter, you will learn more about the technical aspects that you should be evaluating an ICO on.

Their Marketing Strategy

We dealt with this very briefly before, but now it is time for a more in-depth analysis. Like any normal business, the way the product is marketed is going to be a huge factor in its overall success. When ICOs were still a novelty item, and there was hardly any competition, and great marketing was not essential.

Nowadays, however, companies must clearly state their unique selling proposition and give a detailed plan of how they are going to market the product and who they are going to market it to. Not all ICOs lay this strategy out in black and white so you may need to go looking for it.

Look at the following to get clues if the company does not lay out their strategy.

Target Customers

The more time the company spends defining who their target market is, the better they are able to focus their marketing efforts and so the better the results they will get. If they don't have this clearly defined and want to be all things to all people, their efforts will be seriously diluted.

Think of it this way, if you were to shoot at an intruder with a shotgun, some of the pellets would hit them, but they wouldn't have much of an impact on them. A single shot from a .45 would be a lot more effective. The same is true of a marketing strategy. The company must define the core market clearly and then advertise to them. They must advertise in spaces that the target audience is most likely to see it.

Is The Product And Unique Selling Point Clearly Defined?

What do you understand the product to be? Do you understand how it is going to work? Do you feel that the

USP is a good one? If you don't, there's a good chance that other investors will have an issue with this as well.

Sales And Marketing Strategy

How are they going to make sure that the right people are exposed to the product? Where are they going to advertise? What are they going to do to drive sales? What media will they use in the process? The clearer and more detailed the plan, the higher the chances are that they have done their homework properly, that the business will succeed, and that they will be able to attract other investors as well.

How Popular Is The ICO On The Web?

We all used to hate those popularity contests at school, but it is a sad fact of life that the more popular an ICO is, the higher the chance that people will invest in it. This should not be the main criteria that you judge the ICO on, though. Popularity, especially in this game can be fleeting at best. However, it will give you an idea of how many people know about the project and are talking about the project. There are two easy ways to evaluate popularity – Alexa and Google Trends.

Alexa

You can check a site out by going to Alexa.com. You will initially get a seven-day free trial but will need to start paying a monthly fee after that, so this is not the cheapest option. The advantage of using Alexa is that you get to see how many people have visited the page and which sites have linked to the page.

The sites that have linked in are extremely important. Are they authority sites or are they a bit dodgy? If the ICO is brand new, skip this step as there won't be enough history for Alexa to work with.

Google Trends

This is a free option and will give you a fair amount of information. If you need to choose between the two, Google Trends gives the more valuable information. It is simple to use and won't cost a penny.

Start by typing in the search term. Like, Ethereum for example.

You will see the following results:

- **Interest Over Time**: This shows you how popular an ICO has been in terms of web searches and is presented in graph format.

- **Interest By Region**: This shows you who has been searching for the same term and what region they are in.
- **Related Topics**: This will give you further search ideas – maybe people are not typing out the full name of the ICO.
- **Related Queries**: This shows you what similar queries there have been.

What really makes Google Trends a cool tool is that you can compare results side-by-side. So, do your search for your first ICO as normal. You then just hit the compare button and run that search. The information displayed is the same, but the company popularity for both companies will be on one graph, making analysis much easier.

Social Signals

How the company gets its message out there is important. What social media platforms do they work on? Is their branding consistent throughout or do they just slap something together without worrying about how it will look or not?

Good branding is not a guarantee of success, but it is the mark of a more professional organization. You have to ask yourself what you would prefer – something that has been dashed off in a hurry, or a carefully considered approach.

The unique selling point should also be fairly consistent throughout. While a change in direction may become necessary at one time or another, the company should not constantly be shifting its focus. If it does, the marketing will end up being very ineffective.

You can have a look at the following sites to get a picture of how consistent the ICO has been:

- Token Data.io
- Epicenter.tv
- Coin Fund.io
- CoinDesk.com
- CoinTelegraph.com

You can also keep track of this aspect by checking blogposts and podcasts by the companies and others discussing them.

How To Interpret Social Signals Correctly

Looking at the way an ICO deals with social media tells you a lot about whether or not they are really trying to make a go of it and how serious they are. The most popular social media for ICOs are Slack, Facebook, Telegram, Twitter, Reddit so see if you can follow their social media pages as well.

The first thing that you need to check here is how many engaged followers they have. Please note, I said "engaged followers." That means followers that are active and participate on their social media page. It is possible to buy followers on most social media, so a large following there is not necessarily a good indication of how popular the project is.

An active audience is essential because it keeps the ICO on its toes. People who are interested or excited about the product could also raise potential issues they are concerned about or features that they would like to see added.

You need to check on the activity of both the participants and the ICO itself. A good ICO will update regularly and respond to feedback. They should consider suggestions made to them so that they can tailor the project more exactly to what clients want.

Another aspect to consider is how the developers and team talk about the project. Are they easy to find? Are they considered thought leaders in the field, with an established reputation? What have they been saying about the progress of the project? Be very wary of an ICO if you are not able to trace the team easily. I'm not saying that you need their home address or telephone number, but if they don't come up on any social media or online, that's a red flag.

Investing Signals

What signals should you look for when it comes to investing? What you need to look for can be divided up into two major parts – Investors and Partners.

Other Investors

Have a look at who else has invested in the project. Are there any recognizable smart investors on the list? Has anyone made substantial investments? Do the investors have a good reputation? While you should not always follow everything, a smart investor does because they might also make a mistake if they are interested in a particular ICO it could be a good indication that it is worth looking into yourself.

How excited are the other investors? Have the thought leaders in the industry made any mention of the project? Have they advised people to invest in it? Thought leaders in this sphere that you should look up include Vitalik Buterin. Charles Lee, Bobby Lee, Barry Silbert. Erik Voorhees and Vinny Lingham.

You can look at sites like Angel.co and Crunchbase.com to see what kind of projects top investors are investing in.

Don't just look at well-known investors or people that have invested a lot of money, though – are there investors there that seem to always make the right investment decisions? They are also worth following.

Another area to look at for investment tips are the larger investment consortiums. I must stress that they are also not always infallible but, if they are interested in an ICO, it may be a good indication that it is worth investing in. Some investment consortiums you might want to look at include

<u>Union Square Ventures</u>, <u>Digital Currency Group</u>, <u>Polychain Capital</u>, <u>Pantera Capital</u>.

The Partners

Has the company partnered up with any well-known, reputable companies? This is another good indication that it may be worth investing in. While having a good partner is not a guarantee of success, it can certainly be a great help, especially where they bring in the specialist knowledge that the ICO needs.

Unfortunately, there is no shortcut when it comes to checking who the partners are. Your best bet here is to keep up to date with some of the good cryptocurrency news sites and to check on the ICO's website and in their white paper.

Chapter Summary

In this chapter you have learned:

- Why the company needs a detailed marketing strategy.
- Why they must define their target clients and unique selling proposition carefully.
- How to assess how popular the ICO is online.

- What social signals to look for in a good ICO.
- What investment signals point to this being a good investment.

In the next chapter, you will learn how to invest in your first ICO and how to fund that purchase.

Chapter Twelve: **Getting Down To Business**

In this chapter, you will learn more about how you can start investing in your first ICO and how to fund that purchase.

Okay, you have found the perfect ICO, and you are ready to invest. You are basically saying, "Take my money." Hold your horses for a second; it's not all that easy.

First off, let's talk about the difference between an ERC-20 token and a non-ERC-20 token.

An ERC20 Token

Is a line of code that runs on the Ethereum network. It has predetermined interfaces so that it will run on the system. The token amount is normally set at the outset. The company can work on the coding to allow the token amount to change.

An ERC-20 token is best described as coding that represents a share. Not your traditional share because the rights it affords are not the same, but similar in principle. The token is only worth what the market will pay for it and can be transferred to someone else.

The token is distributed via Smart Contracts on the Ethereum network. A Smart Contract is actually a line of code that will execute as soon as a certain criterion has been met. For example, you send an Ether to exchange for a token, and the contract kicks into gear automatically.

It cannot be changed and cannot be stopped – as long as the criterion has been met, the system will automatically finish the transaction.

A Non-ERC-20 Token

These are tokens that can be run outside of the Ethereum network and programmed as the company wants. These are known as protocol tokens and the rights assigned with them will depend on what the terms and conditions are.

If you are considering one of these tokens, check to make sure that you qualify to buy it. Sometimes the company excludes buyers from specific countries; sometimes they only allow accredited investors or those with a certain currency to buy.

For the purposes of this book, we will assume that you are buying an ERC-20 token. The process for both is basically the same anyway.

What Do I Need To Invest In An ICO?

Your first stop is to check the ICO's website and find out what instructions they have given. They will tell you what wallet they recommend, what addresses you must use and whether or not there are additional terms and conditions.

For example, some ICOs make you take the additional step of registering the tokens to finalize the sale.

What you will need for all transactions:

- A cryptocurrency wallet.
- Ether to fund the wallet.
- An address to send the money to.
- A private key.
- A public key.
- Gas to fund the transaction.

Let's have a closer look at these.

A Cryptocurrency Wallet

This is where you are going to store all that Ether that you are going to buy or, to put it another way, somewhere that you can use your private key.

There are a few different kinds of wallets, but the most popular two are:

- **Software Wallets**: These create an account on your device – laptop, phone, etc. to store the currency in. Basically, think of it as a new folder on the computer, with the Ether being a file stored in it. Examples are Jaxx, MyEtherwallet, and Mist. The downside is that if your computer is hacked, you lose your money. If your computer is stolen, ditto. If you don't create a backup and your computer crashes, you lose access to your funds.
- **Hardware Wallets**: These are stored on your computer but also have dedicated devices but give an additional layer of security. So, instead of just accessing your wallet directly, you also have to enter a pin on the device. This is designed to help protect against keyloggers. Examples are Ledger and Trezor. The downside is that these are not easy to install, and you never know what your private key is as it is stored on the device.

A Private Key

The wallet will usually generate a private key for you to use. This must be kept in a secure place and not shared with anyone. Think of it like the PIN number for your ATM card. If someone has it, they can access all your funds. Unlike with your ATM card, however, if you forget your private key, there is no way to recover it. You will lose access to your funds for good. Do keep it safe.

The private key is used to sign transactions so that they can be put forward for processing.

Your Public Key

Transactions on the blockchain are signed using your private key. You don't want to have to transmit that key, though, because then someone could steal your money. The conundrum then becomes, how does the system verify that the transaction is actually from you?

Your public key is what will be used to verify that the transaction is a valid one. It is generated by your private key and is based on the private key but has a different number. When the transaction is submitted, this public key can be transmitted and used to verify the transaction.

This is done through the solving of complex mathematical equations that use your public key to ensure that the transaction is above board. This is why there may be a delay when transferring funds to buy tokens – the transaction must be verified by a few different nodes in the network.

Your public key is basically your Ethereum address. Give it to those people who want to send you money. No one EVER needs to see your private key in order to send you money.

What Is Gas?

The verification of blocks is known as mining. Currently, on Ethereum, this is done through Proof of Work. The miner's computer processes the equations, and so verifies the transaction. It takes a fair amount of processing power and energy to do this and so miners need to be rewarded for doing the work.

The reward comes in the form of gas. Gas is essentially a transaction fee. It is not quite the same as Ether, but Ether can be exchanged for gas.

It's not all that important to make the distinction. The reason that I bring it up is as a warning. Gas works a lot like gas in the car. If you are out on a drive and run out of gas, the car stops, you don't get to your destination, and what gas you had is wasted.

When processing a transaction, you will be given an estimate of the gas needed to power the transaction. You must ensure that you not only have enough Ether to pay for your investment but also enough to pay for the gas.

Getting Ether

You can buy Ether directly on sites like Bitpanda or CEX.io. You will need to register with them, have your identity verified and then purchase Ether using Fiat currency. You can also buy coins on an exchange like Kraken or Coinbase.

What is important is that you should always transfer the coins bought to your wallet. Never leave them in the exchange and do not buy your tokens directly from the exchange either. Why?

It's simple; an exchange acts in much the same way as a bank does. It essentially treats the funds that you keep in your exchange wallet as money it has borrowed from you. In other words, you don't have the actual currency until you withdraw it.

It will allow you to do transfers on the site but if the exchange is hacked, or if it goes bust, your money is lost, and there is no real recourse for you.

If you are participating in an ICO, you must withdraw the funds from the exchange first. Yes, it is possible to send the money directly but here's why this is a really bad idea.

When you send funds directly from the exchange's account, your account on the exchange is debited, but the address that the funds comes from is the exchange's address. So, even though they are acting on your behalf, they are sending the Ether from their address.

When the smart contract is executed, the exchange becomes the owner of the token. They should transfer the tokens on to you, but what happens if they don't? How do you prove ownership?

An Address To Send The Money To

And now, for the final ingredient – the address. This you will find with the instructions on the ICO's site. Do have a read through the terms and conditions before sending money through. You may only be able to buy at certain times of the day, or there may be further steps to take once you have sent the money through.

To Send The Money

In theory, all you need to do is to choose where to send the Ethers to. In practice, it's a little more complicated than your standard bank transfer. You will need to open up your wallet and type in the address that the money is going to and then send it. (Check on your wallet's website for exact instructions.) It is better to copy and paste the address so that you don't make any mistakes.

Where it becomes more complicated is that you need to ensure that the transaction has gone through. You should click on the transaction to see whether or not it was successful. This could take a little while, depending on how busy the network is. On a side note, the gas that is used does not influence how fast the transaction is processed.

Getting Into Ethereum

There are two ways to get yourself onto the Ethereum network – either downloading the Ethereum software or downloading software that can act as a bridge between you and the network instead. Unless you are a developer and really need full access to the system, the latter option is probably going to suit you better.

For beginners, I suggest installing the Chrome Extension Metamask. It gives you a quick and simple way to access Ethereum without installing the full Ethereum software. All you need to do is to look for it in the Chrome Store and then install it.

Using Metamask

When you open it for the first time, you will be asked to read through and accept all the terms and conditions. It does advise that you sign out of the extension when you are done with the site for security reasons.

Once that is done, you will be asked to create a password that is at least eight digits long. This can be uppercase, lowercase, alpha or numerical characters and, if you like, special characters as well.

After that, the system will give you a set of seed words. Save these words somewhere safe. If you lose your password, you will need them to access your account again.

Where Metamask is really helpful is that it links not only to the Ethereum network but also to several test networks. On the Rinkeby Test Network, for example, you get to play around and get used to how Ethereum works without needing to use real money.

These test networks are a way for designers to try out new dapps or contracts without having to pay for them. I suggest that you look at the test network to see what the Ethereum blockchain does look like.

What I do like about Metamask is that you can link up your wallet with it to make transfers easier. In the top right-hand corner of the app, you will see three lines stacked horizontally. Directly to the left of this is a round icon. Click on that icon to create or import account.

If you already have a cryptocurrency wallet, you choose "import account" and then put in your private key to import it, but you can also use the system to buy directly from Coinbase (only if you are in the United States) and Shapeshift.

It can act both as a browser for Ethereum and as a wallet in itself. My advice, as with any web wallet, is to store only as much as you plan to use in there. Transfer the excess to your primary wallet as soon as possible.

Now that you have had a chance to see what things look like, you are ready to start participating in ICOs. You should have read through all the terms and conditions and have gotten the address to send the funds through to so all you need to do now is to make sure that you are active in the main Ethereum network by selecting the correct network in the top left-hand corner.

From there, you just send the funds, wait to see that the transaction is successful and then wait for your tokens to arrive. It's easy once you know how.

Chapter Summary

In this chapter you have learned:

- What an ERC-20 token is.
- What a non-ERC-20 token is.

- That you need to have a cryptocurrency wallet, Ether to fund it, a private key, a public key, an address to send the money to and extra Ether or gas to pay for the transaction to be done.
- The different types of wallets and which are the most secure.
- Gas on the Ethereum network is what fuels transactions. In the same way that your car will stop if it runs out of gas, so will your transaction. Also, like the gas in your car, the gas used up until that point is burnt and not recoverable.
- How to fund your wallet and how to use those funds to invest in an ICO.
- How to access the Ethereum blockchain.
- What Metamask is and how it makes browsing Ethereum and conducting transactions easier.

In the next chapter, you will learn you more about what a crowd sale is and about ways to keep yourself safe from fraudsters wanting to divert your funds.

Chapter Thirteen: Keeping Yourself Safe From Fraudsters

In this chapter, you will learn more what a crowd sale is and also what signs to look out for so that you don't fall victim to fraudsters.

To start off with, most ICOs will set up a crowd sale contract on the Ethereum network. This contract will lay out when people get their tokens, how much each token will cost, whether or not there are restrictions on buying tokens, etc.

So, let's say that I decided to start my own ICO and I called it ICO Fake. Let's also say that I intend to sell as many tokens as I can for ten hours every day for the next week.

You come along and decide to invest in ICO Fake. You would need to make sure that you send through the Ether during the ten-hour period on any of the days that I am selling tokens.

As long as the timing is right, the contract takes over from there. It has a look at how many Ether you have sent, works out how many tokens to send back to and sends the tokens on. All a crowd sale contract is, is a smart contract.

If it is triggered, it will work as it is meant to in terms of its programming. It won't forget to do something, won't make any changes. It will do exactly what it is supposed to do. There is no intermediary to delay the execution and no way of stopping it once it has been triggered.

So, There Is Nothing To Worry About At This Stage?

From the actual ICO's side, no. As long as you send the money to the right address, you are going to get your tokens. However, fraudsters are bound to try to get at your money through a phishing scam.

Basic Phishing Scam To Get Your Private Number

Here is your typical kind of phishing scam. They send out what looks like a legitimate email from the company that handles your wallet. They come up with an excuse for you to check your wallet balance.

Perhaps they ask you to check your balance because they detected unauthorized access to your account. Maybe they'll say they are having a problem with their systems and need you to go in and confirm that all your coins are still there.

Whatever excuse they use, they will have a link to click. The address on the link will be very similar to the main website but not exactly the same. If you do click through to it, you are likely to come up with a site that looks absolutely legitimate. If you do sign in, however, they will be able to capture your private key, and your money will be gone.

If you get an email of this nature and are not sure about how valid it is, the best thing to do is to open your wallet as you normally would, without clicking on any links provided in the email.

Phishing Scam To Get Your Money

A phishing scam is the use of electronic means to convince someone to hand over private information. This information then enables the scammer to gain access to bank accounts, money, etc.

The scamming in this case is not typical of phishing, and so it could be more difficult to sniff out. The fraudsters here are not interested in your personal details at all; they just want the money. They are going to work at convincing you to send the money to them.

One way of doing this is to wait until just before the event starts and to send out a notice that the address has changed. They will usually give what sounds like a valid reason – perhaps they will say that the smart contract had a bug in it and they had to start from scratch.

Another trick is that someone on the forum approaches you with a great deal for "early" investors.

In either case, go and check out the company's website to verify that these are legitimate items. If you find that the address is the same on the website as the new address, it might pay to go one step further and contact someone on the team, just to verify that their website has not been hacked.

Your best protection against this kind of scammer is to verify everything. Is it logical that a company would change the address so soon before the sale? If they have, why is it not blasted all over their social media pages?

Keeping an eye on the social media pages for the ICO you are interested in is a good way to find out if something has gone wrong. The scammer is bound to have approached more than one person, and you will often be warned about this in the forum.

If they have managed to hack the website and put on a new address, but the company caught it in time, this is another area where they will put a warning out on social media.

Chapter Summary

In this chapter you have learned:

- That crowd funding sales are usually based on smart contracts. This means that they execute automatically as long as they are triggered. They will execute without any external influence.
- Fraudsters have moved into this space as well.
- They may try to get your private key through phishing.
- They may use a more advanced type of phishing to get you to send the money to their address rather to the company's address.

In the next chapter, we will provide a quick recap of all the sites referenced in this book.

Chapter Fourteen: Your Cheat Sheet Of Sites

In this chapter, I give you a cheat sheet of all the sites that we have referenced when compiling this book. It is worth creating a folder in your browser titled "Crypto" and then bookmarking all these sites.

When Still Testing The Waters, Keep An Eye On These Media Sites
- Epicenter.tv
- CoinFund.io
- CoinDesk.com
- CoinTelegraph.com
- TokenData.io

Also, Keep Track Of What These Groups Invest In
- Polychain Capital
- Union Square Ventures

- Digital Currency Group
- Blueyard Capital
- Pantera Capital
- Blockchain Capital
- Outlier Ventures
- Early Bird

When You Are Ready To Get Started To Look For ICOs To Invest In

- topicolist.com
- coinschedule.com
- icoalert.com
- cryptocompare.com
- smithandcrown.com
- tokenmarket.net

Tools to Gauge Online Popularity

- Alexa.com
- Google Trends

Exchanges Where You Can Buy Cryptocurrencies

- Poloniex
- Bitpanda
- CEX.io
- Kraken
- Coinbase

Chapter Summary

Now you have a quick cheat sheet to refer to when you start to invest in ICOs.

Final Words

That was a pretty intense ride, wasn't it? It is a lot of information to digest but now you know the basics of investing in an ICO, the sky is the limit.

You now know what the hallmarks of a good ICO are, what the telltale signs of amateurs are and how to protect yourself against fraud in this sphere.

All that is left now is for you to dive in and start looking for those great ICOs. I advise that you start off small, at least until you get the hang of things. Don't be fooled into making rushed decisions because of an "I don't want to miss out" mentality.

Sure, you might miss a good deal or two by hanging back and researching the market, but you are also a lot less likely to make expensive mistakes.

There is no need to rush this at all. ICOs are a popular form of fundraising for companies, and it will be around for a while to come.

Get to know how the landscape works, spend some time reading what the experts say and learning as much as possible about this fascinating new investment opportunity.

One final thing? I would really appreciate it if you left a review for this book when you are done.

Thanks so much and I wish you all the best going forward.

Other Ikuya Takashima books available on Amazon:

Cryptocurrency: How I Paid my 6 Figure Divorce Settlement by Cryptocurrency Investing, Cryptocurrency Trading

Ethereum: The Ultimate Guide to the World of Ethereum, Ethereum Mining, Ethereum Investing, Smart Contracts, Dapps and DAOs, Ether, Blockchain Technology

Blockchain: The Ultimate Guide To The World Of Blockchain Technology, Bitcoin, Ethereum, Cryptocurrency, Smart Contracts

Bitcoin: The Ultimate Guide to the World of Bitcoin, Bitcoin Mining, Bitcoin Investing, Blockchain Technology, Cryptocurrency

Ripple: The Ultimate Guide to the World of Ripple XRP, Ripple Investing, Ripple Coin, Ripple Cryptocurrency, Cryptocurrency

Litecoin: The Ultimate Guide to the World of Litecoin, Litecoin Crypocurrency, Litecoin Investing, Litecoin Mining, Litecoin Guide, Cryptocurrency

About The Author

31-year-old Ikuya Takashima is a Software Developer, entrepreneur, investor and author.

Ikuya first entered the world of Cryptocurrency in 2014 when he finally decided to invest in Bitcoin after several years of following the online currency. Ikuya is now a Cryptocurrency expert & enthusiast with an impressive Cryptocurrency portfolio and investments in several Bitcoin & Ethereum startups.

Ikuya's latest venture is to share his knowledge and passion on the world of Cryptocurrencies with the goal of making seemingly complex and intimidating topics simple and easy-to-read.

In Ikuya's spare time he likes to read, travel and spend time with family and friends.